# ADVANCED
# SKATEBOARDING

**PETER MICHALSKI
AND AARON ROSENBERG**

rosen publishing's
**rosen
central**

Published in 2017 by The Rosen Publishing Group
29 East 21st Street, New York, NY 10010

First Edition

**Library of Congress Cataloging-in-Publication Data**

Names: Michalski, Pete. | Rosenberg, Aaron.
Title: Advanced skateboarding / Peter Michalski and Aaron Rosenberg.
Description: First Edition. | New York : Rosen Central, 2017. | Series:
  (Skateboarding Tips and Tricks) | Includes bibliographical references,
  webography and index.
Identifiers: LCCN 2016008875| ISBN 9781477788615 (Library Bound) | ISBN
  9781477788592 (Paperback) | ISBN 9781477788608 (6-pack)
Subjects:  LCSH: Skateboarding--Juvenile literature.
Classification: LCC GV859.8 .M52 2017 | DDC 796.22--dc23
LC record available at http://lccn.loc.gov/2016008875

*Manufactured in China*

# CONTENTS

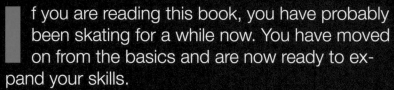

# INTRODUCTION

If you are reading this book, you have probably been skating for a while now. You have moved on from the basics and are now ready to expand your skills.

We'll talk about more advanced skateboarding tricks and give you a host of other useful tidbits— all about how to improve your skateboarding and get the most out of the hobby itself. Whether your ultimate goal is to win competitions and go for the top of your sport as a sponsored skater and champion or simply to challenge yourself and have a great time, building on your basic and intermediate skills is key.

You can rise to the challenge in a variety of skating disciplines and venues—on the street, on street courses, and catching air in bowls and on ramps. By this point, you know yourself and your strengths and skills pretty well. Some skaters are good in every style, while others are better at vert, or street courses. Whatever your pleasure, you can build your skills, whether you want to work on flatland tricks, grabs, grinds and slides, ramp stalls, or much more.

Have patience, take your time, and set your goals. Read on to take your skating skills to new heights!

Professional skater Lizzie Armanto performs a trick in a bowl at the July 2015 Paris Skate Culture event in Paris, France. Getting advanced enough to go pro takes hard work and dedication.

# CHAPTER ONE

# WHERE TO SKATE

**Y**ou may have read about and learned the basics and intermediate skills, perhaps even from this very same book series. Some people have even built up their fundamentals in skating classes. For the most part, you probably have learned skating with friends, from videos online, and just by doing it. It's time to reach for bigger things and up your game.

You want to take it further—but where? This may depend on your local resources and environment. You can skate on the street, in parking lots, and in empty office parks during off hours. Different settings will help you learn different styles.

Luckily, you are living in a time when many towns and cities have recognized the popularity of skating and have invested in skater-friendly development. More than ever before, skate-parks and courses, with street course obstacles, bowls, and ramps, are being built and enjoyed.

You are past basic safety and tricks, and you are raring to go. What are the places you can rise to your new challenge of becoming an advanced skater? Which is best for you, and which style of skating do you want to really concentrate on?

# RAMPS

If you haven't dealt with ramps yet, you probably will—most skateboarders do. That doesn't mean you have to use ramps, but you should at least know what they are and how they work, and try them to see if that type of skateboarding is for you.

You've seen ramps, of course, but what are they, exactly? Half-pipes, bowls, quarter-pipes, and hips all help skateboarders catch air. Most ramps are made from plywood, although some people use Masonite on the surface of the ramp (which is very smooth but can get too slick if wet and tends to get dusty).

If you have a half-pipe near you—whether it belongs to someone you know or is part of local skatepark—it can be a valuable resource to really experience a whole new world of skating.

Ramps are concave (arced inward). They can vary in size and shape, although a good ramp is at least twelve feet wide and can be anywhere from one foot to fourteen feet high. So why are they curved? The curve of a ramp launches you high in the air, where you can do a number of different tricks. The higher you go, the more complex tricks you can do.

## MINI-RAMPS AND VERT RAMPS

Mini-ramps and vert ramps are both half-pipes. They have two opposing walls to help skaters launch air tricks by going back and forth from one wall to the other. Mini-ramps are smaller versions of the vert ramp. They can range from about two to eight feet high. The most popular height is between six and eight feet. The mini-ramp is designed to do more technical tricks (i.e. a lot of flips and turns) whereas the vert ramp is designed to catch air.

The vert ramp is a specially built half-pipe that curves upward into a vertical incline. It is called a vert ramp after the word "vertical." The vertical part of the ramp launches skaters high into the air to do any number of tricks. A vert ramp is at least nine feet tall, where the steepest section of the ramp, near the lip, is vertical (straight up and down). Vert ramps used in competition are at least eleven feet—nine and a half feet of transition and a foot and a half of vert. Transitions are any parts of the ramp that are curved. Skaters need at least those sixteen inches of vert to get their boards completely vertical while still on the surface of the ramp. This sends them straight up and allows them to come straight down and against the vert wall to gain speed that will send them up the opposite ramp. Get it? Speed and vert are the name of the game!

Skate legend Tony Hawk shows his stuff on the vert ramp at Mission Valley YMCA's Krause Family Skatepark during the Sonic Generations of Skate at Clash of Clairemont 7, on June 1, 2013 in San Diego, California.

## OTHER RAMPS

The bowl ramp, or bowl, is as its name suggests, a ramp with concave transitions all the way around, like a giant mixing bowl. A quarter-pipe is a ramp with only one concave transition. It is one half of a half-pipe or mini-ramp, hence the name quarter-pipe, and can be anywhere from one foot to fourteen feet high. Quarters are good for small practice areas (like a driveway or parking lot). If you put two quarters together, facing each other, you'll have a half-pipe with the ground being the flat transition area.

A hip ramp is made up of two launch ramps or quarter-pipes at an angle from one another and touching at one corner.

The angle is called the hip because it juts out like a hip. A variety of creative tricks can be done on a hip ramp.

Some ramps also have escalators—that's where part of the lip, the top edge of the ramp, is not horizontal but slopes from one height to another

Different skateparks (and backyards!) have different ramps.

## SPONSORSHIP

Most skateboarders dream of being sponsored—having a company pay you to skateboard professionally. What could be better for a skateboarder? You get a board with your name and design on it. You get to travel around the world, you get to skate full-time, and somebody pays for it. Sponsorship is hard to get, though. There are hundreds of professional skateboarders and many more thousands upon thousands of amateurs, many competing for sponsorship. So how can you get sponsorship?

The first thing you need to do is to become a very good skater. Then you have to show it off by winning competitions. This will make you known. Sponsors will then hear about you. Of course, there is a bit of luck involved. A lot of luck comes from timing: pro skaters move from one company to another, leaving a spot open on their team. And if you're really lucky, and really good, some day one of those companies may offer to sponsor you. Then all that extra work will have been worth it.

Most follow these basic types. You'll need to practice a bit to decide which ramps you prefer. It's best to work your way up—start with a mini-ramp, then a vert ramp. That way you've got time to get more comfortable on the board—and in the air.

## STREET OR PARK?

So which will it be, street or park? Let's consider the differences.

Street skating is more spontaneous and more immediate. Often, you never know what obstacles you'll find riding street, so you take them as they come. Park skating, in contrast, has all the ramps, rails, and stairs set up. You know exactly what ramps you'll find there, and all of them are specifically made for skaters. In street skating, you're improvising, using existing objects as ramps and rails. These include handrails, concrete benches, lawn borders, and different kinds of stairs. Street obstacles are not built for skating so they are more challenging—and more risky!

Street skating is also more open. You start as soon as you skate out the front door, and you don't stop until you get back home. The world is your skatepark! You can skate in one spot for hours or move from spot to spot as you see fit. There aren't any lines, and you don't have to buy tickets and wait your turn. In a skatepark, you often have to pay to get in, then wait patiently for your turn at whatever ramp or rail you want to skate.

It sounds like street skating is the better option, doesn't it? But let's look at the other side.

Skateparks maintain their equipment. You know the ramps and rails are in good repair and are not going to break on you—or under you. When you're street skating, no one's checking to see if that box is sturdy or rotten or whether there are rusty nails or not.

Skateparks have people to supervise the skaters. That does mean you're being watched, but it means everyone else is, too. If someone cuts you off on a ramp, he or she will get pulled aside. And if you get hurt, there's someone there to take care of it right away. If you're street skating and get hurt, you may have to limp back home yourself before you can get any medical attention.

Skateparks are built specifically for skateboarders. You're welcome there, which means no one will hassle you. You're there to skate, and so is everyone else. When you're street skating, you may get yelled at, or even chased away, because you're in people's way. Some cities and towns even have strict and compli-

In Oregon, Portland's famous Burnside Skatepark was started by skaters, and the city government eventually approved the space officially. It has been featured in video games and feature films.

cated municipal codes against skating in certain areas. The last thing you need is to get a warning, a fine, or even, in some rare cases, arrested, when all you want to do is skate.

Skateparks also give you a place to meet other skateboarders. You can exchange stories, trade tips, learn new tricks, and generally make friends. When you street skate, you might find other skaters but you might not.

So does that mean skateparks are better? As with everything in life, you have to weigh your options and choose what's right for you. What are you interested in? Street skating and skating where you want (and thus taking your chances with the authorities or disgruntled homeowners and business proprietors) may appeal to your sense of freedom and even an appetite for risk-taking. But there remain risks. You may instead want or need more stability and structure as a skater.

What else are you looking for in skating? Do you want to be social and make friends, too, or to get time to yourself?

Sometimes, these decisions are made for you. For example, you may not have a skatepark or course near you and will have to just deal with the street. Whatever works for you and meets your needs is what will be best.

# CHAPTER TWO

# SKATEBOARDING TRICKS

Skateboarding tricks fall into a few categories—some of them even fall into multiple ones. Breaking down the sport into styles of skating and trick styles is an important way to prepare yourself to learn them.

## TRICK TYPES

Let's say you're practicing a 50-50 grind, and then you want to move on and try a 5-0 grind. They're both grinds, so you know they have some features in common. That makes it easier for you to learn the second one because you already have an understanding of the basic principles. Otherwise, you'd have to learn how to do a grind all over again before you could work on the 5-0.

It also helps to know your own strengths and weaknesses. Some people are really good at grabs. Others are better at stalls. Which are you? If you know you're good at grabs, you can concentrate on those more to show off your skills. If you know you're weak on stalls, however, you can look for more advice on those tricks and get in more practice time to improve.

It also helps when talking to others. Just like with naming a trick—if you're comparing notes with another skater you don't want to say, "I can do this one trick where I jump up in the air and bring the skateboard with me." You want to say, "I know

## GETTING INJURED

Skaters get hurt, just like all athletes in demanding sports. Let's face it—skateboarders twist and turn and leap and land, all on a small piece of wood with small wheels under it. They are bound to get hurt sometimes.

The most common injury for skateboarders is a sprain: ankle, knee, wrist, elbow, shoulder—any of the body's joints. Doctors often recommend the R.I.C.E. method for treating sprains:

R-Rest: Stay off your feet whenever possible and try not to use the sprained joint.

I-Ice: Icing the joint during the first twenty-four hours after the injury does two things—it numbs it, which helps reduce pain, and it controls swelling to help the healing process.

C-Compression: Wrap the joint with some sort of dressing or bandage, but not too tightly. You need to let the joint breathe, but you want to hold it still.

E-Elevate: When sitting or lying down, try to keep the joint higher than your chest to keep it above your heart. This keeps the blood from rushing to the joint, which helps reduce the swelling and the pain.

the ollie already." That way you both know what you're talking about. The same is true with types of tricks. If you can say, "Hey, are you any good at airs? I've been having a hard time learning those," you both know what you're talking about, and you're more likely to get useful advice, tips, and even shared stories. That doesn't mean you have to shove each trick into a neat little box and label it, but it helps to discuss what you're doing and to have a name everyone else will recognize.

A skater takes a spill from a failed jump attempt. It is really not a question of if, but when, when it comes to taking a fall. Preparing yourself with safety gear is the best takeaway here.

Here are the basic trick types and styles:

## GETTING OFF THE GROUND: FLATLAND

These are tricks that don't use any inclines—you skate on the ground or some other flat surface. "Flatland skating" and "street skating" are terms that are used interchangeably. That doesn't mean your board stays flat on the ground, but you don't need ramps or anything else, besides the ground and possibly obstacles.

## GRABS

These tricks involve using either hand to grab somewhere on your deck while you are in the air. They can be done on both the street and on ramps.

## GRINDS/SLIDES

These tricks involve moving the bottom of your board or the trucks along the edge or top of an object.

## STALLS

These tricks are done on curbs, railings, or ramps. They involve getting your board into a sliding or

A skater grinds on a handrail. This kind of structure exists both in regular parks, office parks, and skateparks.

grinding position without actually doing a slide or grind—in other words, they focus on balancing your board on something for a few seconds without moving forward and then pulling off the object.

## VERT

This is a style of skating performed on vert ramps, specifically tricks that are performed while in the air.

There are other categories of tricks. Some people invent their own, and not only established, famous, or legendary skaters. The important thing is to be familiar with the territory, know which tricks are related, and what simple skills you need to nail before you can move on to more complicated and difficult ones.

# CHAPTER THREE

# LOW ADVANCED TRICKS

**B**efore moving on to any of the beginning advanced or low advanced tricks, you should have nailed your basics. That is, you should known how to ollie and nollie, do kickflips, and do a pop shove-it. These get you ready for the next tier of skating.

The tricks in this book are divided into three categories: low, medium, and high. That's not the amount of height you need for each trick, it's how difficult they are compared to each other. Low advanced tricks are the least difficult advanced tricks to learn—they're harder than the basic tricks but not by much. Start with these and work your way up, making sure you've mastered each trick before you move on to the next one. Some of them require that you can do easier tricks as well.

## DOING MANUALS

A manual is a trick that lets you ride balancing on your back wheels only.

1. Push off and put your front foot in the middle of the board and your back foot on the tail.
2. Push down on the tail and bring the front wheels off the ground. Balance and hold this position. Try to not have your tail drag on the ground—you want the front wheels just off the ground, but that's it.
3. When you slow down or lose your balance, put the front wheels on the ground and ride off.

You can also do a nose manual—that's when you ride on only your front wheels. To do a nose manual, you put your front foot on your nose and your back foot in the middle of the board. Now just push down with your front foot until the back wheels are off the ground. Be careful not to push down too hard on the nose or you could wind up flipping over!

## THE 50-50 STALL

This closeup shows a skater doing a manual, a fairly simple move that is not only fun but helps you learn balance for other tricks.

Before you try a 50-50 stall, you need to be sure you can do ollies and 180 ollies.

1. Start out by approaching the curb or ledge, straight on, at a medium speed.
2. Before meeting the obstacle, ollie and turn 90 degrees. Now you are in the air waiting to land on the object.
3. Land with both trucks on the edge of the object. Keep your weight centered and balance on the board—you might want to lean forward a little to keep from falling.
4. Now stall—this means you hang there. This isn't a grind, so you're not supposed to be moving along the object.
5. When you're ready to come out of the stall, hit your tail, ollie, and turn away from the object. Land and ride away.

This skater just did a nose stall on a quarter-pipe, one of several tricks that demand balancing on the lip of a ramp.

# LEARNING BOARD SLIDES

When you're first learning the board slide, find an obstacle no higher than your knees. You can work you way up to larger obstacles later, after you've mastered the basics. You'll need to know how to ollie to do this trick.

1. Approach your target at an angle and at medium speed. Don't go too slowly or your board will fail to slide on the object.
2. When you're next to the obstacle, do a 90-degree ollie onto it so that the side of the board is facing forward. Keep

This skater is doing a rail slide in the middle of the skateboard, the board straddling the obstacle perpendicular to its length.

your shoulders perpendicular to the obstacle. It helps to focus on the middle of your board as you slide, so you can keep balanced.

3. Land balanced on the obstacle. Your board should slide forward.

When you're ready to get off, just turn your body and feet the way you want to get off. If the obstacle has a corner or lip in the way, you may need to angle up to get clear. (Note: This is a difficult trick for some people. Don't give up.)

## LIVING ON THE EDGE: GRINDS

In order to grind, you need to know how to ollie. Pick a ledge with coping as your target. The corner of a curb works fine.

1. Approach at a good speed from a shallow angle— you'll need some momentum to grind. Make sure your front foot is by the back bolts on the front truck.
2. Ollie high enough for both trucks to be on the ledge, then push the nose down so the front truck is on the ledge.

A skater grinds across a skatepark obstacle. In a grind, the trucks, and not the wheels or board itself, are the part of the board that are making contact with the environment.

3. Now push forward to grind. You need to keep your balance slightly forward so the board grinds along.
4. When you start to slow down or you reach the end of the ledge, lean back a little, lift the front truck off, and turn away. The back truck will follow.

## BONELESS

1. Start out with your front foot just behind the front truck bolts.
2. Now reach down with your front hand and grab the toe edge of the board in front of your back foot.
3. Take your front foot off the board and slam it onto the ground behind you (on the heel side). Use this to jump off the ground, keeping the board under you with your front hand. In the air, turn 180 degrees and land fakie (with the tail of your board going forward).

**PIONEERING SKATERS**

**Want to be famous? Invent a trick!**
   Here are a few examples of notable skaters and the moves they came up with.

   In the eighties, Eric Dressen tilted his 5-0 grinds a bit toward bluntslides, dubbed this move the salad grind, and made history.
   Sal Barbier thought Brian Lotti's last name sounded a bit like "lottery," so he dubbed one of Lotti's tricks "the

big spin," after a scratch ticket in California.

Neil Blender invented the frontside air backside grab (in back of the front foot) and dubbed it the lien air. "Lien" is "Neil" spelled backward. (According to Blender, though, you have to "lien" (lean) in to make it.)

Mike Smith was the first to pull off a particular grind— back truck on, front truck below coping. Now it's called the Smith grind.

Josh Kasper took the benihana to another level by including a stare down in midair. That's now called a Kasperhana.

Blasting out of a vert ramp, with arms and legs sticking out to form a "T," and pulling it was something that only Christian Hosoi could do. Now it's called a Christ air.

Duane Peters invented the sweeper. It's called that because it looks like you're sweeping the deck.

Alan Gelfand aired out of a pool, frontside, without using his hands, changing skateboarding forever. Now it's called an ollie.

Steve Caballero was the first one to spin a fakie 360 air, without grabbing. Not surprisingly, it's called a Caballerial now.

Tony Hawk and Lester Kasai decided to come up with a new trick. They figured they needed a catchy name if the trick was going to be a hit, so they named it the Madonna after the singer. Apparently it worked.

# RAMP IT UP: KICK TURNS

The kick turn is a ramp trick, so you'll need a mini-ramp or a vert ramp.

1. First, ride up the transition until you reach just below the lip.
2. Now shift your weight to your back foot and let the front wheels lift off the surface.
3. Push down on the board with your back foot and turn your chest to face the flat bottom at the same time.
4. Now push down on the front again so the wheels touch the ramp, and ride back down.

Dropping into a half-pipe, bowl, or pool is a must-have skill for anyone who wants to progress in his or her skating.

# DROPPING IN

To do tricks in a half-pipe, you must first know how to drop in. Dropping in gives you speed and sets you up for all half-pipe tricks. First, find a small half-pipe. A three- or four-foot half-pipe is good to learn on.

Place your tail on the coping, so your trucks and wheels hang over the edge. Put your back foot on the tail and your front foot right behind the front bolts. Keep your weight on your back foot.

Now lean forward and shift enough weight to your front foot for the front truck to lay on the ramp. Be careful to balance! If you don't put any weight back on the tail after you lean in, you'll simply flip over. You also don't want to put everything onto the tail as you go down or you'll flip up instead and the board will shoot out from under you.

Keep both trucks on the ramp as you ride down to the flat bottom.

# CHAPTER FOUR

# MEDIUM ADVANCED TRICKS

Once you have learned the low advanced tricks, there's nowhere to go but up. Those should give you the basic skills to move on to the medium advanced tricks in this chapter. Time to ramp it up yet again!

## ROCK 'N' ROLL

This is a ramp trick, so you should be comfortable dropping in.

1. Drop in.
2. On your way up to the opposite coping, keep your back foot on the tail and your front foot on the first two bolts of the front truck.
3. Push down on your tail so your nose lifts and your front trucks reach over the coping.
4. Then, stall the board on the lip in a board-slide position, but not moving.
5. After a few seconds place your weight on the tail so that the front trucks lift back over the lip.
6. Lift the nose high enough to clear the lip and ride back into the ramp fakie. Make sure your front truck doesn't get caught on the coping.

7. Push down slightly with your front foot so your front truck is back on the ramp and roll down fakie.

## GETTING SOME AIR

The air described here is a vert trick.

1. Ride up the transition, and as you rise above the lip in the air, reach to grab the board. You can grab the board any way you wish. You need to grab the board to have it stay beneath your feet.
2. Start to turn. It is easier to turn backside (with you chest facing the flat bottom) when first learning this trick.
3. Once you've finished turning, and your nose is facing toward the flat bottom, let go of the board as it passes below the coping and push hard against the ramp as soon as possible. Once all four wheels are planted on the surface of the ramp, slowly straighten out your legs as you ride down the transition.

## FLIPPING THE SCRIPT: HEELFLIPS

The heelflip is basically the same trick as a kickflip except that you flip the board in the opposite direction by using your heel.

1. Put your feet in the ollie position, but with your

The steps of a heelflip are covered here from beginning to end (from right to left). Skater Rodney Mullen is credited with inventing it.

toes hanging over the edge of the front of the board.
2. Now ollie. Once your board levels out in midair, push down on the toe side of the board so that it flips.
3. After one complete flip, land on the board and ride away.

## INDY GRAB

This is a fairly simple grab, so it's a good way to start learning this type of trick.

1. Move forward slowly on a flat surface. Now ollie as high as you can, bending your knees as much as possible since you have to be able to reach the board with your hand.

The basic kind of grab to do is an indy grab. From this grab, most others follow, and it can performed off or on ramps, on rails, or from the ground.

2. At the top of your ollie, grab the toe side of your board with your right hand (left hand if you're goofy). Hold the grab until you're about to touch the ground.
3. Let go of the board, bend your knees to absorb the shock, land, straighten up, and ride away.

## MUTE GRAB

A mute grab is when you grab the toe side of the board with your left hand (right hand if you skate goofy-footed).

1. Ollie and grab your board while you're in the air. If you're doing an ollie off a ramp or some other obstacle, you should grab your board and hold it. If you're just skating flatland and ollie off the ground, you should grab the board briefly and let go.
2. As you come down, release the board before you land.

## TAIL GRAB

This grab is less difficult since it's easier to reach the tail.

1. Ollie as high as you can.
2. Crouch down and grab the tail with your right hand (left hand if you skate goofy).
3. Let go of the tail and ride away. It's important that you quickly let go of the tail or you'll have trouble landing.

## HALF-CAB

Before you try a half-cab you should be comfortable with ollies and fakie ollies. Learn how to land the half-cab before doing it

## WHAT'S IN A NAME?

As we have touched upon, many tricks get their names from the skaters who came up with them, whether they are named after them or incorporate jokes or wordplay. Skate legend Steve Caballero originally invented the Caballerial, combining his name and "aerial," which is a 360-degree turn from a fakie, usually performed on vert ramps. Thus, a half-cab is half a Caballerial; namely, a 180-degree turn.

A skater is shown in midair doing a backside half-cab 180.

over obstacles.

1. Ride fakie on a flat surface and ollie.
2. Rotate 180 degrees.
3. Land with the nose going forward and roll away.

# CHAPTER FIVE

# HIGH ADVANCED TRICKS

**A**fter getting a good deal of practice with the low advanced and harder medium advanced tricks, it's time to aim high with the high advanced tricks. It is important that you have nailed a good deal of the less complex maneuvers first. Otherwise, you might have a pretty tough time and even risk hurting yourself. Advanced tricks often combine two (or even more) easier tricks.

## DOING A VARIAL FLIP

The varial flip is a combination of a kickflip and a 360-degree pop shove-it.

1. Put your front foot in the kickflip position (similiar to an ollie, but with your front foot hanging off slightly, toward the edge of your board) and your back foot in the pop shove-it position
2. Now kick with your back foot as if you were going to do a 360-degree pop shove-it.
3. As the board starts to rotate, flip the board with the toes of your front foot as you would a kickflip. The

board should be spinning like a pop shove-it and a kickflip at the same time.

4. For the complete trick, the board should spin 360 degrees and flip once, both at the same time. If done right, the board will spin so fast that it will be hard to judge when it is in the upright position to land. You must develop a feel for when the right time to land is. This trick is all about timing. Stay over the board and land it with your feet over the trucks.

# OLLIE IMPOSSIBLE

This one is tough to learn, so don't give up if you can't get it at first.

1. Roll along at a comfortable speed on a flat surface. Place your front foot right in front of the nose. Your back foot should be on the tip of the tail, and your toes should hang off the tip of it.
2. Now snap the board like an ollie
3. Here's the tricky part! Don't move your front foot forward to even the board out. Instead, slide your front foot off the board.
4. Now sweep your back foot under you and make the board flip around your back foot. The board will flip backward 360 degrees, touching your back foot the whole time.
5. After the board finishes rotating, bring your front foot back to tip the board so it's no longer flipping around on its side.
6. Now land with the board under your feet.

At the beginning, you might want to practice flipping

the board around your back foot with your front foot on the pavement.

## LANDING HANDPLANTS

This is another ramp trick.

1. Ride up the transition and grab the board with your front hand just below the lip. Reach out with your back hand, and plant it on the lip.
2. Ride up beyond the ramp and grab the lip so your arm pushes your body straight up into the air. Your position is now basically a one-handed handstand, while holding your board with your free hand.
3. Now pull your body toward your arm and let go of the lip.
4. Fall back to the ramp and ride back down.

Tony Hawk does a hand plant at the lip of a ramp as photographers snap pictures of the vert skating legend.

## GETTING INJURED . . . ACCORDING TO THE PROS

The first time you get hurt, you'll probably say, "I guess I'm not cut out for this skateboarding stuff." Why not? Do you think that only amateurs get hurt?

The truth is, everyone gets hurt—skateboarding is risky, and you *will* fall down. Most falls happen while you're learning a new trick.

Josh Kasper says that injuries happen all the time, and the only thing you can do is rest up, use the downtime to plan ahead, and get back to the skateboard once you're healed. His worst injury happened when he was in Mexico—he wound up with three fractures, a chipped heel, a pulled hamstring, and a nerve injury.

Tony Hawk admits he gets scrapes, sprains, and bruises all the time, and he says you just learn to live with it.

Steve Caballero says it comes in spurts for him; he won't get hurt for a while and then suddenly he'll get hurt all the time. His worst injury was a broken ankle.

Mike Vallely says he gets hurt daily, and every few years he's injured severely and has to take time off to heal. His worst injury was a torn shoulder muscle.

Donny Barley's worst injury was a rolled ankle, complete with torn ligaments.

Charlie Thomas's worst injury involved three broken bones—all in one foot!

All the pros agree on some points. First off, when you're injured you need to rest up. Don't go hopping back on the skateboard after a day or two—wait until the doctor says it's OK. If you go back too soon, you may not heal fully, and that injury could bother you for the rest of your life.

Also, keep busy while you're hurt. Read, watch videos, play on the computer, catch up with family and friends. Don't lose touch with skateboarding, either—keep track of what's going on, check out websites and read magazines, and generally keep informed. They also say that yes, after being injured you may be nervous skateboarding again—especially on the trick that knocked you down. But you have to get back up there and start riding again. The more time you spend back on your board, the stronger your confidence will get and the more comfortable you'll be again. Hey, if it works for the pros, it'll work for you!

## DEFYING GRAVITY: WALLRIDES

To do this trick, you need to be able to ollie at least two feet off the ground.

1. Ride toward a wall at a 45-degree angle. You want to ride

Wallrides are one of the gravity-defying tricks you can look forward to attempting as you get better and better.

the board facing the wall. Get ready to ollie at the wall, and keep your eyes on the spot you want to wallride.

2. Ollie up, but don't level out. Instead, bring your back foot up in line with your front foot while pushing the board toward the wall. Push your heels forward and your toes back. The board should be parallel to the ground.

3. Now snap your toes forward, pushing the board up against the wall. You only want the balls of your feet on the board while you're wallriding, otherwise you won't be able to stay upright. If you do this right, you should be able to ride the wall for a second or two.

4. To get off a wallride, bend your legs a little (if they aren't already).

5. Pop the tail and jump away from the wall.

6. Now level out the board with your hand by pulling your wrist in. Keep your feet flat against the deck.

7. Extend your legs a little to absorb the impact, land, and ride off.

**bowl ramp** A ramp with concave transitions all the way around, like a giant mixing bowl.

**flatland** A trick that makes no use of any inclines, and you skate on the ground or some other flat surface.

**grab** A trick that involves either hand grabbing somewhere on your deck while you are in the air. It can be done on both the street and on ramps.

**grind** A trick involving moving the trucks of your board along the edge or top of an object.

**half-pipe** A ramp with two opposing walls. It dips down in the middle and back up on either side.

**hip ramp** Two launch ramps or quarter-pipes at an angle from one another and touching at one corner. The angle is called the hip because it juts out like the part of the body.

**mini-ramp** A small half-pipe.

**park skating** Skating in a skatepark, using ramps and surfaces specifically designed for skateboarding.

**quarter-pipe** A ramp with only one concave transition.

**ramp** A curved or inclined surface built to let skateboarders perform tricks in midair.

**slide** This is a trick that involves moving the bottom of your board along the edge or top of an object.

**stall** A trick that involves balancing your board on something for a few seconds without moving forward and then pulling off the object.

**street skating** Skating without using any ramps or anything but found obstacles.

**trick** A particular maneuver you learn to do while skateboarding.

**vert** This is a style of skating performed on vert ramps, specifically tricks that are performed while in the air.

**vert ramp** A specially built half-pipe that curves upward into a vertical incline.

Go Skateboarding Foundation
22431 Antonio Parkway
Rancho Santa Margarita, CA 92688
(949) 455-1112
Website: http://goskateboardingfoundation.org
The Go Skateboarding Foundation provides education, career
    programming, and scholarships, and helps fund skateparks.

Harold Hunter Foundation
151 First Avenue
New York, NY 10003
Website: http://haroldhunter.org
The Harold Hunter Foundation, named after an iconic New York City
    skater and actor, is a grassroots, community-based organization
    that uses skateboarding as an outreach tool, encouraging skat-
    ing among urban youth as a path to confidence, empowerment,
    and skill-building.

International Skateboarding Federation (ISF)
P.O. Box 57
Woodward, PA 16882
(814) 883-5635
Website: http://www.internationalskateboardingfederation.com
The International Skateboarding Federation (ISF) is formally orga-
    nized and incorporated to provide direction and governance
    for the sport of skateboarding worldwide.

Skatepark Association of the United States of America (SPAUSA)
2210 Lincoln Boulveard
Venice, CA 90291
Website: http://www.spausa.org
The Skatepark Association of the United States of America
(SPAUSA) is a nonprofit organization that assists communities
in obtaining the resources to build their own skateparks.

Skaters for Public Skateparks
820 North River Street, Loft 206
Portland, OR 97227
Website: http://www.skatepark.org
Skaters for Public Skateparks is a nonprofit advocacy group
that provides information to those hoping to finance, build,
and/or improve their local skateparks and other skating
venues.

## WEBSITES

Because of the changing number of Internet links, Rosen Publishing has developed an online list of websites related to the
subject of this book. This site is updated regularly. Please use
this link to access this list:

http://www.rosenlinks.com/STT/advan

Caitlin, Stephen. *Skateboard Fun*. Mahwah, NJ: Troll Communications, 1988.

Choyce, Lesley. *Skateboard Shakedown*. Halifax, Canada: Formac, 1989.

Christopher, Matt, and Paul Mantell. *Skateboard Renegade*. New York, NY: Little Brown and Company, 2000.

Goodfellow, Evan, and Doug Werner. *Street Skateboarding: Endless Grinds and Slides: An Instructional Look at Curb Tricks*. Chula Vista, CA: Tracks Publishing, 2005.

Irvine, Alex, and Paul Parker. *So You Think You're a Skateboarder?: 50 Tales from the Street and the Skatepark*. New York, NY: CICO Books, 2014.

Lombard, Kara-Jane, ed. *Skateboarding: Subcultures, Sites, and Shifts* (Routledge Research in Sport, Culture and Society). New York, NY: Routledge, 2015.

Marcus, Ben. *The Skateboard: The Good, the Rad, and the Gnarly*. Minneapolis, MN: MVP Books/Lerner Publishing, 2011.

Michalski, Peter, and Justin Hocking. *Riding Halfpipes* (Skateboarding Tips and Tricks). New York, NY: Rosen Publishing, 2016.

Michalski, Peter, and Justin Hocking. *Skating Bowls and Pools* (Skateboarding Tips and Tricks). New York, NY: Rosen Publishing, 2016.

Sohn, Emily. *Skateboarding: How it Works* (The Science of Sports–Sports Illustrated for Kids). Mankato, MN: Capstone Publishers, 2010.

Watts, Franklin, and James Nixon. *Skateboarding Champion* (How to Be a Champion). New York, NY: Franklin Watts/Scholastic, 2015.

# BIBLIOGRAPHY

Badillo, Beal, and Dan Werner. *Skateboarding: Book of Tricks (Start-Up Sports)* Chula Vista, CA: Tracks Publishing, 2003.

Beal, Becky. *Skateboarding: The Ultimate Guide*. Santa Barbara, CA: ABC-CLIO, 2013.

Dunham, Dan, with Matthew B Gross, Tim Leighton-Boyce, John Nixon, and Rick Valenzuela. "Skateboarding FAQ, October 1995" (http://web.cps.msu.edu/~dunhamda/dw/faq.html).

Hocking, Justin. *Life and Limb: Skateboarders Write from the Deep End*. New York, NY: Soft Skull Press, 2004.

Mullen, Rodney. *The Mutt: How to Skateboard and Not Kill Yourself*. New York, NY: IT Books/HarperCollins, 2004.

Transworld Skateboarding (http://skateboarding.transworld.net).

Watt, Andy. *Dansworld Ramp Building FAQ* (http://www.cse.msu.edu/~dunhamda/dw/ramp_faq.html).

Wixon, Ben. *Skateboarding: Instruction, Programming, and Park Design*. Champaign, IL: Human Kinetics, 2009.

# INDEX

## A

air, catching, 4, 7, 8, 29

## B

Barbier, Sal, 24
Barley, Donny, 37
basic skills, knowing, 4, 14–18, 19
Blender, Neil, 25
boneless, 24
bowls, 4, 6, 7, 9

## C

Caballerial, 25, 32
Caballero, Steve, 25, 32, 36

## D

Dressen, Eric, 24
dropping in, 27, 28

## E

escalators, 10

## F

50-50 stall, 20–21
flatland tricks, 4, 17, 31

## G

Gelfand, Alan, 25
grabs, 4, 14, 17, 25, 29, 30–31
grinds, 4, 14, 17, 23–24, 25

## H

half-cab, 31–32
half-pipes, 7, 8, 9, 27
handplants, 35
Hawk, Tony, 25, 36
heelflips, 29¬–30
hip ramps, 7, 9–10
Hosoi, Christian, 25

## I

indy grab, 30–31
injuries, 15, 36–37

## K

Kasai, Lester, 25
Kasper, Josh, 25, 36
kickflips, 19, 29, 33–34
kick turns, 26

## L

Lotti, Brian, 24

## ABOUT THE AUTHORS

Peter Michalski is a young adult nonfiction author who has penned many instructional titles for teens, covering sports, careers, and health issues.

Aaron Rosenberg has written role-playing games, educational books, magazine articles, short stories, and novels for White Wolf and the Star Trek: Starfleet Corps of Engineers series. He also runs his own role-playing game publishing company. Aaron lives and works in New York City.

## PHOTO CREDITS

Designer: Michael Moy; Editor: Philip Wolny;
Photo Researcher: Karen Huang and Philip Wolny

# Find the Truth!

**Everything** you are about to read is true *except* for one of the sentences on this page.

Which one is **TRUE**?

**T or F**   Temperatures at the bottom of the canyon are colder than those higher up.

**T or F**   The Grand Canyon is 1 mile (1.6 kilometers) deep on average.

Find the answers in this book.

3

# Contents

## THE BIG TRUTH!

**Bald eagle**

4

The Colorado River in the Grand Canyon

**A hiker**

Be careful! Falling is a serious danger at the Grand Canyon. Never get too close to the edge.

# CHAPTER 1

# A Grand History

As you peer out over the railing, you almost can't believe your eyes. You've seen pictures of the Grand Canyon before, but seeing it for real is so much more amazing! The canyon's walls are lined with colorful stripes of rock. Between the towering walls, far below you, the shining waters of the Colorado River rush along the bottom of the canyon. It is a truly stunning sight!

The Grand Canyon was the 17th national park created in the United States.

★ Grand Canyon National Park

Many people visit Mather Point, a great spot for views of the park.

## Attracting an Audience

Located in northwestern Arizona, the Grand Canyon is one of the most famous natural landforms on Earth. It is known for its incredible views, rich history, and the amazing activities visitors can enjoy there. All this draws huge crowds to Grand Canyon National Park , the 1,904-square mile (4,931-square kilometer) area surrounding the canyon. More than 4.5 million people on average travel there every year from all around the world.

# Billions of Years in the Making

To learn about the canyon's history, you can study the layers of rock that make up its massive, sloped walls. Over very long periods of time, each layer formed on top of the previous one. The layers are made up of different kinds of rocks. This is what gives the canyon its unique striped appearance.

The materials that formed the oldest visible rock layer first settled over 2.5 billion years ago!

Youngest rock layers

Oldest rock layers

About six million years ago, the Colorado River began flowing along its present path from the Rocky Mountains in Colorado to the Gulf of California. The water's movement eventually wore a path in the ground. The Grand Canyon slowly formed over millions of years as the river dug this path deeper and deeper over time. Rain, wind, and other forces also caused the canyon's sides to **erode**. This widened it and made its sides slope downward.

# A Timeline of Grand Canyon Milestones

## 6 million years ago

The Colorado River first flows along its current course through what became the Grand Canyon.

## 12,000 years ago

Humans first move into the Grand Canyon region.

## 600 CE

The Pai, ancestors of the Hualapai and other native groups, first settle along the Colorado River.

# The People of the Canyon

Humans first came to the Grand Canyon about 12,000 years ago. **Archaeologists** have uncovered ancient hunting tools, pottery, and other artifacts in the canyon. Several Native American groups eventually settled in the region. They included the Navajo, the Hualapai, and the Havasupai. Many **descendants** of these groups live near the park today.

**1869**

Explorer John Wesley Powell leads the first U.S. expedition down the river and through the canyon.

**1903**

President Theodore Roosevelt visits the Grand Canyon. He declares it "the one great sight which every American should see."

**1919**

Congress passes a law creating Grand Canyon National Park.

The Grand Canyon became a part of the United States in 1848. It was part of a large portion of land the U.S. government obtained from Mexico as a result of the Mexican-American War (1846–1848). At the time, the land was largely unmapped. Few people outside of the Native Americans who lived there had ever seen the Grand Canyon. European-American explorers began traveling to the new region to study the canyon and the surrounding area.

By the late 1800s, the Grand Canyon had already become a popular tourist attraction. Many people wanted the government to protect the canyon. They knew that too much human activity could ruin its natural beauty. In 1919, Congress voted to make the area a national park. Anyone would be free to visit, but no one would be allowed to own the park's land or build on it.

# National Park Fact File

A national park is land that is protected by the federal government. It is a place of importance to the United States because of its beauty, history, or value to scientists. The U.S. Congress creates a national park by passing a law. Here are some key facts about Grand Canyon National Park.

| Grand Canyon National Park | |
| --- | --- |
| Location | Northwestern Arizona |
| Year established | 1919 |
| Size | 1,904 square miles (4,931 square kilometers) |
| Average number of visitors each year | More than 4.5 million |
| Widest point of the canyon | 18 miles (29 km) |
| Deepest point of the canyon | 6,000 feet (1,829 m) |

A hiker takes in the beauty of the Grand Canyon.

Well-marked trails allow hikers to easily explore the wonders of the Grand Canyon.

# CHAPTER 2

# Exploring the Canyon

The first thing you might notice when you reach the canyon is its remarkable size. It stretches on for 277 miles (446 km) of the Colorado River's length. At its widest point, the canyon spans 18 miles (29 km) between its two rims: the North Rim and the South Rim. From the edges of the rims to the river below, the canyon has an average depth of about 1 mile (1.6 km).

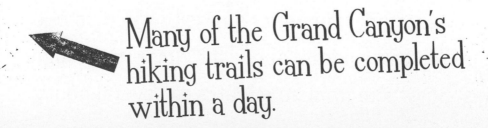
Many of the Grand Canyon's hiking trails can be completed within a day.

The Colorado river flows between the canyon's two rims.

# Getting Around

The South Rim is easy to reach by car and is open year-round. This makes it more popular among visitors. The North Rim is much higher and more difficult to reach, and it closes for several months each winter. Its hiking trails are also more challenging.

Helicopter tours offer an exciting way to peer into the canyon from above the rims. These flights last anywhere from 20 minutes to several hours.

# A Walk in the Sky

The Skywalk is a glass sidewalk that juts out over the Grand Canyon, 4,000 feet (1,219 m) from the bottom. It is located outside the park in nearby lands that belong to the Hualapai. These native people have lived in the region for centuries. In the 1800s, white settlers took over much of their land. The U.S. government gave some land back in 1883. The Skywalk helps attract tourists, which creates jobs and exposes visitors to Hualapai culture and history.

Members of the Hualapai Nation before the Skywalk opening ceremony in 2012.

# Into the Canyon

To enter the canyon itself, many people take a mule ride. Travelers start at one of the canyon's rims. Expert guides lead them to the bottom of the canyon. The entire trip takes about three hours. The journey isn't backbreaking, but it can be rough. The mules travel along pathways carved carefully into the canyon's sloping sides. Along the way, riders see many parts of the canyon that aren't visible from above.

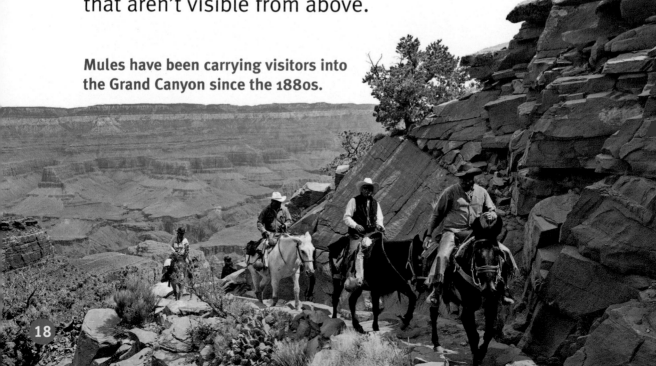

**Mules have been carrying visitors into the Grand Canyon since the 1880s.**

# Hot and Cold

At the Grand Canyon, you need to be prepared for different weather conditions. Up on the rims, summer days are mild and nights are cool. But deeper in the canyon, the temperature is warmer. At the bottom, it can heat up to 120 degrees Fahrenheit (49 degrees Celsius) during the summer. In winter, expect very cold temperatures and snow on the rims. However, the warmth inside the canyon melts snow into rain before it reaches the bottom.

**Even the tallest buildings in the world would fit easily inside the Grand Canyon.**

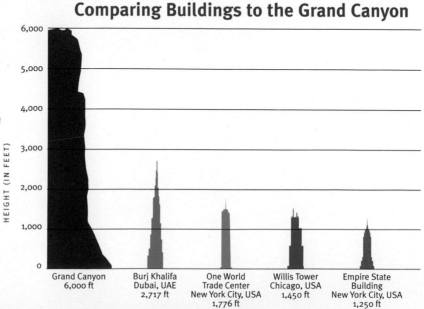

**Comparing Buildings to the Grand Canyon**

HEIGHT (IN FEET)

6,000
5,000
4,000
3,000
2,000
1,000
0

Grand Canyon
6,000 ft

Burj Khalifa
Dubai, UAE
2,717 ft

One World
Trade Center
New York City, USA
1,776 ft

Willis Tower
Chicago, USA
1,450 ft

Empire State
Building
New York City, USA
1,250 ft

STRUCTURES

Bring your binoculars to enjoy incredible bird-watching at the Grand Canyon.

# CHAPTER 3

# Creatures Great and Small

As you explore the Grand Canyon, you'll be amazed at the variety of animals you see. Thousands of **species** populate the canyon, from enormous birds to tiny insects. Spotting these animals is one of the coolest parts of visiting the park. However, you should always remember to leave the animals alone. Don't try to feed them, touch them, or even get too close!

Grand Canyon National Park is home to nearly 450 bird species.

California condors can glide for hours looking for carrion, or dead animals, to eat.

# Up in the Air

Birds of all kinds are a common sight in Grand Canyon National Park. They range from tiny, insect-eating wrens to huge birds of prey such as bald eagles. The park is even home to the California condor. This is one of the most **endangered** bird species in the world. Its enormous wingspan measures about 9.5 feet (3 meters) across.

# Magnificent Mammals

More than 90 **mammal** species roam throughout the park. Small animals such as squirrels and ringtails scurry across tree branches. Bats soar through the night sky. Larger animals such as mule deer, elk, and bison are also easy to find. Mountain lions stalk the park's deer and elk, as well as its smaller mammals. When driving on the park's roads, visitors should keep an eye out for these big cats. They are sometimes hit by cars.

Mountain lions are also known as catamounts, cougars, panthers, pumas, and other names.

# Creepy Crawlers

More than 1,440 insect and other **invertebrate** species also live in the park. You might spot butterflies flapping their colorful wings or bees dashing among wildflowers. Huge black beetles crawl across the ground. There are even tarantulas! Enormous and hairy, you'll most likely see these oversize spiders in fall when they leave their burrows to find mates. And while a tarantula bite is not dangerous, make sure to avoid another arachnid, the bark scorpion.

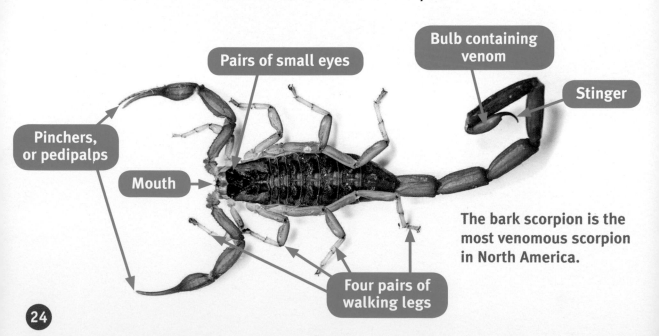

Pairs of small eyes

Bulb containing venom

Stinger

Pinchers, or pedipalps

Mouth

Four pairs of walking legs

The bark scorpion is the most venomous scorpion in North America.

A fisher grabs a rainbow trout from the river.

## Creepers, Leapers, and More

Many other kinds of animals can also be found in the park. Reptiles are very common. These include colorful lizards, slow-moving tortoises, and deadly rattlesnakes. Near the Colorado River or other water sources, you will likely spy frogs, toads, and other amphibians. If you wade in a little deeper, you might also find some of the park's five **native** fish species.

# National Park Field Guide:
# Grand Canyon

Here are a few of the hundreds of fascinating animals you may see in the park.

## Canyon tree frog

**Scientific name:** *Hyla arenicolor*

**Habitat:** Near streams in forested areas, usually perched on rocks and boulders

**Diet:** Ants, spiders, beetles, flies, and other small invertebrates

**Fact:** The inside of their back legs is bright yellow, which can only be seen when the frogs jump.

## Mojave rattlesnake

**Scientific name:** *Crotalus scutulatus*

**Habitat:** Open rocky areas in the canyon, but sometimes on the rims

**Diet:** Small animals, including mammals, birds, and reptiles

**Fact:** The snake's rattle is mostly used to scare away possible attackers.

## Gila monster

**Scientific name:** *Heloderma suspectum*

**Habitat:** Desert areas in westernmost parts of the park

**Diet:** Rodents, lizards, bird eggs, and invertebrates

**Fact:** A gila monster's bite is venomous and painful.

## Mule deer

**Scientific name:** *Odocoileus hemionus*

**Habitat:** The entire park

**Diet:** A range of plants, such as grass and shrubs, nuts, and berries

**Fact:** The mule deer's range extends from Mexico all the way to Alaska.

## Desert bighorn sheep

**Scientific name:** *Ovis canadensis nelsoni*

**Habitat:** Steep areas and cliffsides

**Diet:** Grasses and shrubs

**Fact:** These sheep can perch comfortably on a ledge as little as 2 inches (5 centimeters) wide.

## Bald eagle

**Scientific name:** *Halliaeetus leucocephalus*

**Habitat:** Usually near water sources

**Diet:** Fish and smaller birds

**Fact:** Bald eagles aren't really bald. They're named for the white feathers that cover their heads.

# From Forest to Desert

Grand Canyon National Park is most famous for its dramatic rock formations. But it is also home to an incredible variety of plants. Weather conditions and the availability of water vary significantly throughout the park. As a result, there are dramatic changes in the types of plants you see as you explore different areas. You'll find heavily wooded forests, grassy meadows, sparse deserts, and more.

More than 2,000 plant species can be found in Grand Canyon National Park.

Pinyon pines and juniper trees grow along the edges of the North Rim.

Aspen leaves in fall

# Tremendous Trees

Forests probably aren't what you picture when you think of the Grand Canyon. However, they are exactly what you'll find up high on many parts of the North and South Rims. Most of the trees are evergreens, such as spruce, fir, and pine. But one deciduous, or non-evergreen tree, stands out. Each fall when the leaves change, bright yellow leaves of the quaking aspen attract visitors to the North Rim.

# Hidden Meadows

If you explore the North Rim, you might be lucky enough to see one of the park's few meadows. These beautiful areas are covered in a thick blanket of tall green grasses. They are found high up in the same areas where forests grow and water is plentiful. Different grasses grow in these areas depending on how much water is available.

About a dozen plant species in Grand Canyon National Park cannot be found anywhere else.

# Down in the Desert

Fruit

Spine

Pad

Three basic parts of a prickly pear cactus

As you travel farther down into the canyon, the landscape starts to look more like a desert. The weather is hotter here, and there is less water. The landscape is dotted sparsely with a variety of bushes. You'll also see plenty of cacti. These spiky plants thrive in hot, dry environments. When it rains, they soak up as much water as possible and store it for later use.

**A redbud tree blooms along the Colorado River inside the canyon.**

## Along the Riverbanks

If you make it all the way down to the banks of the Colorado River, you'll see a whole new group of plants. Many types of trees, shrubs, and wildflowers can be found here. You might also see leafy ferns. These ancient plants likely first appeared in the Grand Canyon as long as 400 million years ago. This is before any of the other types of plants found there today had begun to grow on Earth.

A Grand Canyon National Park ranger inspects the park.

# CHAPTER 5

# Protecting the Park

National parks are protected by a variety of laws. These regulations are designed to preserve the parks' wildlife and natural beauty. However, the Grand Canyon still faces environmental challenges. For example, many of the area's animals are **threatened** or endangered, such as the California condor. For others, including some fish species, it is already too late. They have disappeared from the park.

The park is home to eight threatened or endangered animal species.

Tamarisk grows behind native grasses along the Little Colorado River.

# Unwanted Invaders

Invasive species pose a serious threat. These are plants and animals that are not native to the park. When they spread into a new area, they upset the environment's natural balance. Tamarisk is an invasive shrub that people brought to the Grand Canyon in the early 20th century to fight erosion. The plant spreads quickly, however, and crowds out native plants. Park workers now remove many tamarisk plants in an attempt to control their spread.

Wild donkeys, called burros, were once a damaging invasive species in the park. After decades of effort to control the burro population, few remain there.

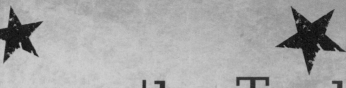

# Safety on the Trail

Park rangers have a challenging job in preserving the park. Much of this work involves making sure the park's hundreds of trails remain safe for visitors exploring the Grand Canyon. Weather can cause rockslides, crumbling paths, and other safety hazards. Park employees watch constantly for these dangers. Rangers close down trails, post warnings, and make repairs as necessary. This helps ensure that visitors do not get hurt as they enjoy the park. Rangers also work to educate visitors about other potential hazards, such as not drinking enough water while hiking.

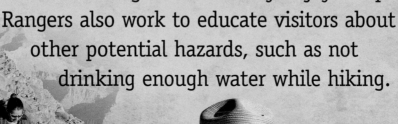

# Restoring Rare Species

There are many ongoing efforts to protect the park's threatened and endangered species. For example, there were only nine wild California condors alive in 1983. Wildlife experts captured them and began raising their young in **captivity**. Beginning in the 1990s, these captive-raised condors were released into the wild near the Grand Canyon. Today, the total wild California condor population in Arizona and California has risen to more than 400. This includes almost 170 that currently live in captivity.

California condor populations have grown in recent years.

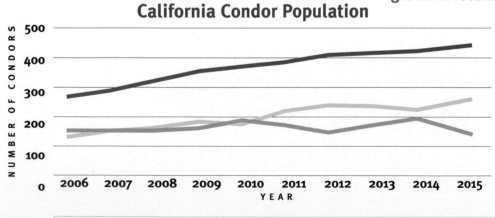

**California Condor Population**

NUMBER OF CONDORS

YEAR

**KEY**
Total Condor Population  Wild Condor Population  Captive Condor Population

City lights can affect areas that are miles away.

## People Problems

Increased human population around the Grand Canyon over many years has led to more cars, power plants, and other sources of air pollution. Mining operations threaten to pollute the Colorado River. Electric lights affect the park's nighttime views of the starry sky. Low-flying aircraft bring loud, unfamiliar sounds. These problems have no easy solution. But people can help the environment generally with simple steps like conserving water and electricity. With everyone's help, we can preserve the Grand Canyon and other places of natural beauty. ★

# Map Mystery

At the end of a trail sits a simple-looking building designed as a place for visitors to take a break and enjoy the view. What is the building called? Follow the directions below to find the answer.

Skywalk

Colorado River

A R I

Co

Ya

### Directions

1. Start at South Entrance Station.

2. Head north to Park Headquarters.

3. Travel east until you reach the Desert View Visitor Center.

4. Now hike west along the South Rim, following the Colorado River.

5. Almost there! West of Grand Canyon Village, look for a spot where you can take a rest—and solve the mystery!

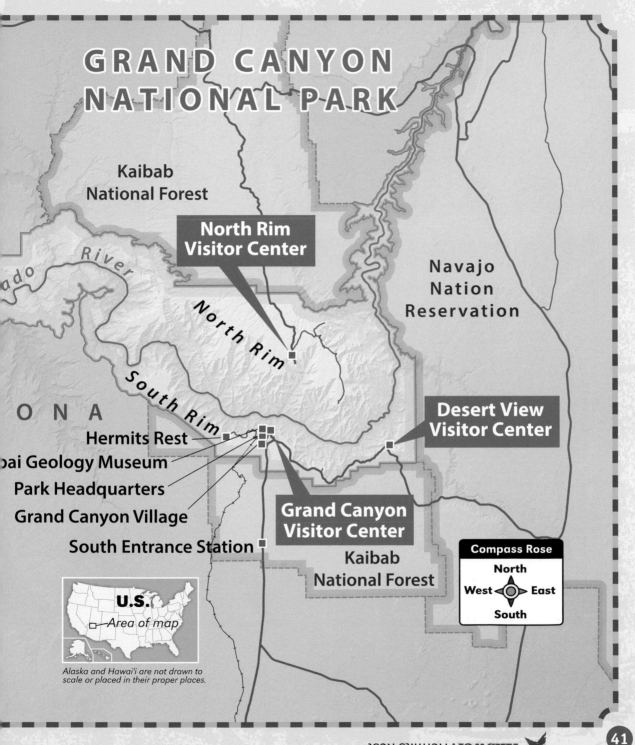

# GRAND CANYON NATIONAL PARK

Kaibab
National Forest

**North Rim
Visitor Center**

North Rim

Navajo
Nation
Reservation

Colorado River

South Rim

ON A

Hermits Rest

bai Geology Museum

Park Headquarters

Grand Canyon Village

South Entrance Station

**Desert View
Visitor Center**

**Grand Canyon
Visitor Center**

Kaibab
National Forest

**U.S.**
Area of map

Alaska and Hawai'i are not drawn to
scale or placed in their proper places.

**Compass Rose**
North
West — East
South

# Be an Animal Tracker!

If you're ever in Grand Canyon National Park, keep an eye out for these animal tracks. They'll help you know which animals are in the area.

### Bison
**Hoof length:** 5 inches (13 cm)

### Mountain lion
**Paw length:** 3 inches (8 cm)

## Elk

**Hoof length:** 3 inches (8 cm)

## Mule deer

**Hoof length:** 3 inches (8 cm)

## Bighorn sheep

**Hoof length:** 3 inches (8 cm)

## Ringtail

**Paw length:** 1 inch (3 cm)

# True Statistics

**Length of the Grand Canyon:** 277 mi. (446 km)

**Total length of the Colorado River:** 1,450 mi. (2,333 km)

**Width of Grand Canyon at its widest point:** 18 mi. (29 km)

**Number of plant species in the park:** More than 2,000

**Number of bird species:** Nearly 450

**Number of mammal species:** 91

**Number of reptile species:** About 48

**Number of amphibian species:** About 10

**Number of known insect and arachnid species:** More than 1,440

## Did you find the truth?

**F** Temperatures at the bottom of the canyon are colder than those higher up.

**T** The Grand Canyon is 1 mile (1.6 kilometers) deep on average.

# Resources

## Books

Flynn, Sarah Wassner, and Julie Beer. *National Parks Guide U.S.A.*
Washington, DC: National Geographic, 2016.

O'Connor, Jim. *Where Is the Grand Canyon?* New York: Grosset &
Dunlap, 2015.

Rowell, Rebecca. *The 12 Most Amazing American Natural Wonders.*
North Mankato, MN: 12-Story Library, 2015.

**Visit this Scholastic website for more
information on Grand Canyon National Park:**
★ www.factsfornow.scholastic.com
Enter the keywords **Grand Canyon**

# Important Words

**archaeologists** (ahr-kee-AH-luh-jists) people who study the distant past by digging up and examining its physical remains, such as old buildings, household objects, and bones

**captivity** (kap-TIV-i-tee) the condition of being held or trapped by people

**descendants** (di-SEN-duhnts) one's children, their children, and so on into the future

**endangered** (en-DAYN-jurd) in danger of becoming extinct, usually because of human activity

**erode** (i-ROHD) to wear away gradually by water or wind

**expedition** (ek-spuh-DISH-uhn) a long trip made for a specific purpose, such as for exploration

**invertebrate** (in-VUR-tuh-brit) relating to an animal without a backbone

**mammal** (MAM-uhl) a warm-blooded animal that has hair or fur and usually gives birth to live babies

**native** (NAY-tiv) living or growing naturally in a certain place

**species** (SPEE-sheez) one of the groups into which animals and plants are divided; members of the same species can mate and have offspring

**threatened** (THRET-uhnd) vulnerable, facing the possibility of becoming endangered

# Index

Page numbers in **bold** indicate illustrations.

# About the Author

Josh Gregory is the author of more than 100 books for kids. He has written about everything from animals to technology to history. A graduate of the University of Missouri-Columbia, he currently lives in Portland, Oregon.